WOMEN ARE FROM VENUS, MEN ARE FROM HELL

WOMEN ARE FROM VENUS, MEN ARE FROM HELL

Amanda Newman

POCKET
BOOKS

LONDON • SYDNEY • NEW YORK • TOKYO • SINGAPORE • TORONTO

First published in the USA by
Adams Media Corporation, 1999
This edition published by Pocket Books, 2002
An imprint of Simon & Schuster UK Ltd
A Viacom Company

1 3 5 7 9 10 8 6 4 2

Simon & Schuster UK Ltd
Africa House
64-78 Kingsway
London WC2B 6AH

www.simonsays.co.uk

Simon & Schuster Australia
Sydney

A CIP catalogue record for this book is available
from the British Library

ISBN 0-7434-6096-0

Typeset by SX Composing DTP, Rayleigh, Essex
Printed and bound in Great Britain by
William Clowes Limited, Beccles and London

I'd like to thank Christine, Mom and Dad, Craige and Bruce, the readers and editors who helped me pick the best stuff, and to women everywhere who love men in spite of what jerks they can be.

My Heart — A light hearted look at the Man woman Condition all my love

Maya

Contents

There Must Be Some
    Misunderstanding   *1*

Women: Smarter Because
    They Have To Be   *21*

Men: Simple or Just Dense?   *39*

'Til Death . . .   *63*

This Is Equality?   *89*

Lowlifes   *99*

Total Slams   *111*

Guys On Guys   *123*

The Secret Lives of Men   *141*

The Sex Part   *167*

Fear of the 'C' Word   *187*

Can't Live With 'Em . . .   *197*

THERE MUST
BE SOME
MISUNDERSTANDING

If you can't live without me, why aren't you dead yet?

—*Cynthia Heimel*

~

Women have considerable moral sense when they don't love a man. Mighty little when they do. With men, it's the opposite. If he doesn't care for a girl, he's without scruples. If he does care, he is likely to develop a moral code only the angels can live up to.

—*Mark Reed*

They say women talk too much. If you have worked in Congress you know that the filibuster was invented by men.

—*Clare Boothe Luce*

~

The most sympathetic of men never fully comprehend woman's concrete situation.

—*Simone de Beauvoir,*
The Second Sex

Why are women . . . so much more interesting to men than men are to women?

—*Virginia Woolf,*
A Room of One's Own

~

When women are depressed, they eat or go shopping. Men invade another country. It's a whole different way of thinking.

—*Elayne Boosler*

If men liked shopping, they'd call it research.

—*Cynthia Nelms*

~

A 'woman driver' is one who drives like a man and gets blamed for it.

—*Patricia Ledger,*
New York Tribune

Ever since Eve gave Adam the apple, there has been a misunderstanding between the sexes about gifts.

—Nan Robertson,
New York Times

~

Women are not forgiven for ageing. Robert Redford's lines of distinction are my old-age wrinkles.

—Jane Fonda

Behind every great man there is a surprised woman.

—*Maryon Pearson*

~

If a man speaks in the forest and there is no woman to hear him, is he still wrong?

—*George Carlin*

~

There aren't any hard women, just soft men.

—*Raquel Welch*

To really know a man, observe his behaviour with a woman, a flat tire and a child.

—*Anonymous*

~

Like many other women, I could not understand why every man who changed a nappy has felt impelled, in recent years, to write a book about it.

—*Barbara Ehrenreich,*
New York Times

When a woman is very, very bad, she is awful, but when a man is correspondingly good, he is weird.

—*Minna Antrim,* Naked Truths and Veiled Allusions

~

Men and women, women and men. It will never work.

—*Erica Jong,* Fear of Flying

Men and children . . . think that if you're sitting down it means you're waiting for someone to give you something to do.

—*Serena Gray,*
'Beached on the Shores of Love'

~

Why dogs are better than men:
Dogs do not play games with you – except fetch (and they never laugh at how you throw).

—*Anonymous*

I got divorced recently. It was a mixed marriage. I'm human, he was Klingon.

—*Carol Leifer*

~

He may be fat, stupid and old, but none the less he can condemn the woman's flabby body and menopause and encounter only sympathy if he exchanges her for a younger one.

—*Liv Ullmann*

From my experience of life I believe my personal motto should be 'Beware of men bearing flowers'.

—*Muriel Spark,*
Curriculum Vitae

~

The real trouble about women is that they must always go on trying to adapt themselves to men's theories of women.

—*D.H. Lawrence,*
Fear of Flying

He said he'd call me the next day, but in boy time that meant Thursday.

—*Amy Heckerling,* Clueless

~

Man to woman: 'I'm not ignoring you – you've got my full peripheral attention.'

—*Stephanie Piro,* Fair Game

Announcing:
SEMINARS FOR MEN
COURSE 005:
We Do Not Want Sleazy
Underthings For Christmas

—Anonymous

~

What men really mean: 'Of course
I like it, honey, you look beautiful.'
Really means . . . 'Oh, man, what
have you done to yourself?'

—Anonymous

Face it: love isn't like it is in the movies. Walt Disney and Doris Day lied to us. I want my money back.

> —*Jann Mitchell,*
> Codependent For Sure

~

The main reason guys will never admit to having even the teensiest clue about what women really want is because if they did, they'd have to *do something about it.*

> —*Barbara Graham*

A woman can walk through the Louvre Museum in Paris and see 5,000 breathtaking paintings on the wall. A man can walk through the Louvre Museum in Paris and see 5,000 nails in the wall. That is the inherent difference.

—*Erma Bombeck*

~

Few men are happy saying, 'I don't know'. They prefer, 'That's not what's important here'.

—*Anonymous*

I don't think the woman has been born to whom it would occur to substitute sports equipment lined up next to the wall for furniture groupings and area rugs. And yet I have frequently visited the 'home' of a man who thought this was a fine idea.

—*Merrill Markoe,* What The Dogs
Have Taught Me

~

If high heels were so wonderful, men would be wearing them.

—*Sue Grafton*

Sometimes I wonder if men and women really suit each other. Perhaps they should just live next door and just visit now and then.

—*Katherine Hepburn*

~

Women will sometimes admit making a mistake. The last man who admitted that he was wrong was General George Custer.

—*Matt Groening*

INDIFFERENCE: a woman's feeling toward a man, which is interpreted by the man as 'playing hard to get'.

—*Anonymous*

~

Most women are introspective: 'Am I in love? Am I emotionally and creatively fulfilled?' Most men are outrospective: 'Did my team win? How's my car?'

—*Rita Rudner*

For some reason, it is universally regarded as fascist to say 'So?' to a woman who has just told you how she feels.

— *Roy Blount, Jr*

~

If you believe everything between women and men is hunky-dory, then you probably don't need this book. Also, you should return to your own planet because you've grown dangerously light-headed.

— *'Jake'*, Glamour

WOMEN: SMARTER BECAUSE THEY HAVE TO BE

Don't accept rides from strange men, and remember that all men are as strange as hell.

—*Robin Morgan,*
Sisterhood Is Powerful

~

The average girl would rather have beauty than brains because she knows that the average man can see much better than he can think.

—Ladies Home Journal

Every man who is high up loves to think that he has done it all himself; and the wife smiles, and lets it go at that. It's our only joke. Every woman knows that.

—*Sir J.M. Barrie,*
What Every Woman Knows

~

If the right man does not come along, there are many fates far worse. One is to have the wrong man come along.

—*Letitia Baldrige,*
Of Diamonds and Diplomats

A woman has got to love a bad man once or twice in her life, to be thankful for a good one.

—*Marjorie Kinnan Rawlings,*
The Yearling

~

The old theory was: 'Marry an older man because they're more mature.' But the new theory is: 'Men don't mature. Marry a younger one.'

—*Rita Rudner*

Personally, I think if a woman hasn't met the right man by the time she's twenty-four, she may be lucky.

—*Deborah Kerr*

~

As long as you know that most men are like children, you know everything.

—*Coco Chanel*

~

Men have sight; women have insight.

—*Victor Hugo*

25

Getting along with men isn't what's truly important. The vital knowledge is how to get along with one man.

—*Phyllis McGinley*

~

God gave women intuition and femininity. Used properly, the combination easily jumbles the brain of any man I've ever met.

—*Farrah Fawcett*

A man on a date wonders if he'll get lucky. The woman already knows.

—*Monica Piper*

~

Even the wisest men make fools of themselves about women, and even the most foolish women are wise about men.

—*Dr Theodore Reik,*
The Need To Be Loved

The only time a woman can really
succeed in changing a man is
when he is a baby.

—*Natalie Wood*

~

I married beneath me;
all women do.

—*Nancy Astor,*
Dictionary of National Biography
1961–1970

Any smart woman will tell you that the best way to a man's heart is through his ego.

—*Anonymous*

~

Men were only made into 'men' with great difficulty even in primitive society. The male is not naturally 'a man' any more than the woman. He has to be propped up into that position with some ingenuity and is always likely to collapse.

—*Wyndham Lewis*

Going to a male gynaecologist is like going to a mechanic who doesn't own his own car.

—Carrie Snow

~

A wise woman puts a grain of sugar into everything she says to a man, and takes a grain of salt with everything he says to her.

—Helen Rowland

What passes for woman's intuition is often nothing more than man's transparency.

—*George Jean Nathan*

~

First time you buy a house you see how pretty the paint is and you buy it. The second time you look to see if the basement has termites. It's the same with men.

—*Lupe Velez*

Dancing is wonderful training for girls; it's the first way you learn to guess what a man is going to do before he does it.

—Christopher Morley

~

If a man is vain, flatter. If timid, flatter. If boastful, flatter. In all history, too much flattery never lost a gentleman.

—Kathryn Cravens,
Pursuit of Gentleman

All discarded lovers should be given a second chance, but with somebody else.

—Mae West

~

How can you tell the difference between men's real gifts and their guilt gifts? Guilt gifts are nicer.

—Anonymous

Us country women make good
wives. No matter what happens,
we've seen worse.

—*Keith Jennison*

~

Every mother knows that her most
spoiled child is her husband.

—*Walter Winchell*

A woman doesn't care what a man looks like. They'd rather a man wouldn't be handsome, so he'll think about them instead of about himself.

—David Graham Phillips

~

Some women know that if they want a man made right, they'd better make him themselves.

—Denis Boyles, A Man's Life

All men are jackals, but you need one to protect you from the rest of them.

—*Marlene Dietrich*

~

You see a lot of smart guys with dumb women, but you hardly ever see a smart woman with a dumb guy.

—*Erica Jong*

It's a man's world, but women are running it, secretly.

—*Cheri Oteri*

~

A man cannot ditch a woman, because she feels it – she knows it's coming.

—*Sinbad*

~

The only man a girl can depend on is her daddy.

—*Grease*

Searching for a boy in high school is like searching for meaning in a Pauly Shore movie.

—*Amy Heckerling,* Clueless

~

A girl can wait for the right man to come along but in the meantime that still doesn't mean she can't have a wonderful time with all the wrong ones.

—*Cher*

MEN:
SIMPLE OR
JUST DENSE?

Men are stupid and women are crazy. And the reason women are so crazy is because men are so . . . stupid.

—*George Carlin*

~

I'm not denyin' the women are foolish: God Almighty made 'em to match the men.

—*George Eliot,*
Adam Bede

What's with you men? Would hair stop growing on your chest if you asked directions somewhere?

—*Erma Bombeck,* When You Look Like Your Passport Photo, It's Time To Go Home

~

The man who thinks he has no faults has at least one.

—*Anonymous*

There are two periods in a man's life when he doesn't understand a woman. Before marriage and after marriage.

—Anonymous

~

I told someone I was getting married, and they said, 'Have you picked a date yet?' I said, 'Wow you can bring a date to your own wedding?' What a country!

—Yakov Smirnoff

What men really mean: 'I'm going fishing.' Really means . . . 'I'm going to drink myself dangerously stupid, and stand by a stream with a stick in my hand, while the fish swim by in complete safety.'

—*Anonymous*

~

If it weren't for women, men would still be wearing last week's socks.

—*Cynthia Nelms*

Why dogs are better than men:
Dogs are happy with any video
you choose to rent, because they
know the most important thing is
that you're together.

—*Anonymous*

~

Blessed is the man who, having
nothing to say, abstains from giving
us worthy evidence of the fact.

—*George Eliot*

If men can run the world, why can't they stop wearing neckties? How intelligent is it to start the day by tying a little noose around your neck?

—*Linda Ellerbee*

~

A man who correctly guesses a woman's age may be smart, but he's not very bright.

—*Anonymous*

Men are very confident people. My husband is so confident that when he watches sports on television, he thinks that if he concentrates he can help his team. If the team is in trouble, he coaches the players from our living room, and if they're really in trouble, I have to get off the phone in case they call him.

—*Rita Rudner*

Women make fools of some men.
Other men are the do-it-yourself
type.

—*Anonymous*

~

There are three things most men
love but never understand:
females, girls and women.

—*Anonymous*

Next to the striking of fire and the discovery of the wheel, the greatest triumph of what we call civilization was the domestication of the human male.

—*Max Lerner,*
The Unfinished Country

~

I love the male body, it's better designed than the male mind.

—*Andrea Newman,* Today

These are some sure-fire ways to tell if your date is too young for you. Can he fly for half fare? Are his love letters written to you in crayon? Is his bedroom wallpapered in a clown motif? Do his pyjamas have feet? When you ask him a question, does he raise his hand before answering?

—*Phyllis Diller*

~

A woman's guess is much more accurate than a man's certainty.

—*Rudyard Kipling*

Most men are boys. Men who are men are probably best, but almost impossible to find.

—*Cynthia Heimel,* If You Can't Live Without Me, Why Aren't You Dead Yet?

~

Answering 'Who was that on the phone?' with 'Nobody' is never going to end that conversation. Ditto for 'Whose lipstick is this?'

—*Anonymous*

This bugs me the worst. That's when the husband thinks that the wife knows where everything is, huh? Like they think the uterus is a tracking device. He comes in: 'Hey, Roseanne! Roseanne! Do we have any Cheetos left?' Like he can't go over and lift up that sofa cushion himself.

—*Roseanne*

~

I hate women because they always know where things are.

—*James Thurber*

There's nothing so stubborn as a man when you want him to do something.

—*Jean Giraudoux,*
The Madwoman of Chaillot

~

A man usually falls in love with the woman who asks the kind of questions he is able to answer.

—*Ronald Colman*

A man admires the woman who makes him think but he keeps away from her. He likes the woman who makes him laugh. He loves the girl who hurts him. But he marries the woman who flatters him.

—*Nellie B. Stull*

~

Women over thirty are at their best, but men over thirty are too old to recognize it.

—*Jean-Paul Belmondo*

Man: If you were a guy, you'd understand.
Woman: Well, if you had ovaries, you wouldn't be so stupid!

—Suddenly Susan

~

It's relaxing to go out with my ex-wife because she already knows I'm an idiot.

—*Thomas Warren*,
The Quotable Quote Book

Supermarkets are like giant booby traps for males – which is why if you send a man out to buy eggs, sugar and bread you should not be surprised if he returns home with a case of wine, a pair of jeans and a tree.

—*Anonymous*

~

What is the only time a man thinks about a candlelight dinner? When the power goes off.

—*Anonymous*

Next to activities that involve balls of many shapes and sizes, guys love to talk about how they're completely baffled by women.

—*Barbara Graham*

~

Behind every successful woman are several confused men who give her something to make fun of.

—*Sarah Miller*

Could any man ever learn that mystical thing called woman's intuition, which isn't mystical at all but rather an ability to pick up and process subtle clues that men lack because we're kind of dense?

—*Bill Cosby,* Love & Marriage

~

It is impossible to defeat an ignorant man in an argument.

—*William G. McAdoo*

What is the proper answer when the little woman asks the following question? 'Can you tell I've lost weight?' A, Not really. I'd say you'd have to lose another ten pounds before it begins to show. B, If you say so. C, WOW!

—Jean Kerr

~

What is the thinnest book in the world? What Men Know About Women.

—Anonymous

A woman knows all about her children. She knows about dentist appointments and football games and romances and best friends and favourite foods and secret fears and hopes and dreams. A man is vaguely aware of some short people living in the house.

—Matt Groening

~

Announcing:
SEMINARS FOR MEN
COURSE 013:
Reasons To Give Flowers

—Anonymous

A man will wear every article of clothing he owns, including his surgical pants that were hip about eight years ago, before he will do his washing. When he is finally out of clothes, he will wear a dirty sweatshirt inside out, rent a U-Haul and take his mountain of clothes to the laundrette, and expect to meet a beautiful woman while he is there.

—*Anonymous*

Most men don't do laundry because washing machines don't come with remote controls.

—*TV ad*

~

I was on a date recently and the guy took me horseback riding. That was kind of fun, until we ran out of quarters.

—*Susie Loucks*

'TiL
DEATH . . .

There is so little difference between husbands you may as well keep the first.

—*Adela Rogers St Johns*

~

Never trust a husband too far nor a bachelor too near.

—*Helen Rowland*

Marriage is an attempt to change a night owl into a homing pigeon.

—*Anonymous*

~

It isn't tying himself to one woman that a man dreads when he thinks of marrying; it's separating himself from all the others.

—*Helen Rowland*

Being married was like having a hippopotamus sitting on my face, Mrs Brown. No matter how hard I pushed or which way I turned, I couldn't get up. I couldn't even breathe . . . Hippopotamuses aren't all bad. They are what they are. But I wasn't meant to have one sitting on my face.

—*Faith Sullivan,*
The Cape Ann

You know that the urge for revenge is a fact of marital life.

—*Jane Smiley,* Good Will

~

The only thing that keeps me from being happily married . . . is my husband.

—*Andra Douglas*

~

I used to live alone . . . then I got a divorce.

—*Greeting card*

Any woman who still thinks marriage is a 50-50 proposition is only proving that she doesn't understand either men or percentages.

— *Florynce Kennedy*

~

Mrs Smith said that she could always tell when her husband was lying. If his lips were moving, he was.

— *Anonymous*

Man of few words: one who takes three hours to tell you he is a man of few words; husband.

—*Anonymous*

~

The man who boasts he never made a mistake is often married to a woman who did.

—*Anonymous*

My husband said he needed more space, so I locked him outside.

— *Roseanne*

~

I'd marry again if I found a man who had fifteen million dollars, would sign over half to me and guarantee that he'd be dead within a year.

— *Bette Davis*

If brides, they should be very cautious about asking their husbands to dry the dinner dishes. The right start is important to a marriage. Make them wash 'em right from the beginning.

> —*Georgie Starbuck Galbraith,*
> *'Horoscope for Housewives',*
> McCall's

~

An archeologist is the best husband any woman can have: the older she gets, the more interested he is in her.

> —*Agatha Christie*

I'll tell you the real secret of how to stay married. Keep the cave clean. Sharpen his spear and stick it in his hand when he goes out in the morning to spear that bear; and when the bear chases him, console him when he comes home at night and tell him what a big man he is, and then hide the spear so he doesn't fall over it and stab himself . . .

—*Jerome Chodorov and Joseph Fields,* Anniversary Waltz

Only one woman in ten recognizes her husband as the same man he was before she married him. Nine out of ten say he's changed. One in three says he's changed for the worse.

—*Gallup Survey, 'The Woman's Mind',* Ladies' Home Journal

~

Husbands are like fires. They go out when unattended.

—*Zsa Zsa Gabor,* Newsweek

Fat generally tends to make a man a better husband. His wife is happy in the knowledge she is not married to a woman chaser. Few fat men chase girls, because they get winded too easily.

— *Hal Boyle*

~

All husbands are alike, but they have different faces so you can tell them apart.

— *Anonymous*

If love means never having to say you're sorry, then marriage means always having to say everything twice.

—*Estelle Getty*

~

I've been married to one Marxist and one Fascist, and neither one would take the rubbish out.

—*Lee Grant*

Announcing:
SEMINARS FOR MEN
COURSE 002:
You Too Can Do Housework

—*Anonymous*

~

Marrying a man is like buying
something you've been admiring
for a long time in a shop window.
You may love it when you get it
home, but it doesn't always go
with everything else in the house.

—*Jean Kerr*

A Californian woman says her husband is at the dangerous age when all females look alike to him – desirable!

—*Anonymous*

~

The man who owes it all to his wife seldom pays her back.

—*Anonymous*

~

Eat, drink and re-marry.

—*Post-it notes*

Get a job, your husband hates you. Get a good job, your husband leaves you. Get a stupendous job, your husband leaves you for a teenager.

—*Cynthia Heimel*

~

If a woman laughs at her husband's joke, it means he has told a new joke or he has a new wife.

—*Anonymous*

You can always surprise your husband on your anniversary just by mentioning it.

—*Al Schlock*

~

If we did get a divorce, the only way he would know it is if they would announce it on *Wide World of Sports*.

—*Dr Joyce Brothers*

Divorce? No. Murder? Yes.

—*Anne Hayes*

~

Marriage isn't a 50-50 proposition very often. It's more like 100-0 one moment and 0-100 the next.

—*Billie Jean King*

What men really mean: 'Uh huh',
'Sure, honey', or 'Yes, dear'. Really
means . . . absolutely nothing. It's a
conditioned response like Pavlov's
dog drooling.

—*Anonymous*

~

Husband: How come you never
tell me when you enjoy sex?
Wife: Because you're never home.

—*Joey Adams*

I had only one friend, my dog. My wife was mad at me, and I told her a man ought to have at least two friends. She agreed – and bought me another dog.

—*Pepper Rodgers*

~

When men reach their sixties and retire, they go to pieces. Women go right on cooking.

—*Gail Sheehy*

American husbands are the best in the world; no other husbands are so generous to their wives, or can be so easily divorced.

—*Elinor Glyn*

~

Pretend to treat your wife as a rational creature. It may surprise her at first, but she'll appreciate it. On the other hand, she may burst out crying – thinking you're drunk again.

—*Anonymous*

Marriage originates when a man meets the only woman who really understands him. So does divorce.

—Ohio State Sun Dial

~

All a man expects his wife to be is a sweetheart, a valet, an audience and a nurse.

—Anonymous

Marriage entitles women to the protection of strong men who steady the stepladder for them while they paint the kitchen ceiling.

—*Anonymous*

~

Try praising your wife, even it it does frighten her at first.

—*Billy Sunday*

There are no records to prove it, mind you, but I have every reason to believe my husband was an eleventh month baby. And he's been running two months late ever since.

—*Erma Bombeck*

~

When a party reveller asks, 'Have you ever thought of leaving your husband' and you answer, 'Where?', you're married.

—*Erma Bombeck*

I know what I wish Ralph Nader would investigate next. Marriage. It's not safe, it's not safe at all.

—*Jean Kerr,* Penny Candy

~

'Left Hand' is the hand that every married man in a singles bar keeps in his pocket.

—*Nancy Linn-Desmond*

Men hate to lose. I once beat my husband at tennis. I asked him, 'Are we going to have sex again?' He said, 'Yes, but not with each other.'

—*Rita Rudner*

~

Trust your husband, adore your husband and get as much as you can in your own name.

—*Joan Rivers*

THIS IS EQUALITY?

Whatever women do they must do twice as well as men to be thought half as good. Luckily, this is not difficult.

—*Charlotte Whitton*

~

Ginger Rogers did everything that Fred Astaire did. She just did it backwards and in high heels.

—*Variously attributed to Faith Whittlesey, Linda Ellerbee and Ann Richards*

Like every good little feminist-in-training in the sixties, I burned my bra – and now it's the nineties and I realize Playtex had supported me better than any man I've ever known . . .

—Susan Sweetzer

~

When a woman demands equal rights, she is simply indulging in flattery.

—Anonymous

I have yet to hear a man ask for advice on how to combine marriage and a career.

—*Gloria Steinem*

~

I'm furious about the Women's Liberationists. They keep getting up on soapboxes and proclaiming that women are brighter than men. That's true, but it should be kept quiet or it ruins the whole racket.

—*Anita Loos*

If you want something said, ask a man; if you want something done, ask a woman.

—*Lady Margaret Thatcher*

~

Women who seek to be equal with men lack ambition.

—*Timothy Leary*

~

A woman without a man is like a fish without a bicycle.

—*Gloria Steinem*

Whether women are better than men I cannot say – but I can say they are certainly no worse.

—*Golda Meir*

~

If men could get pregnant, abortion would be a sacrament.

—*Florynce Kennedy*

Some men think they have an inferiority complex, when, in fact, they are just inferior.

—*Anonymous*

~

I don't mind living in a man's world as long as I can be a woman in it.

—*Marilyn Monroe*

There is very little difference between men and women in space.

—*Helen Sharman, astronaut*

~

A man can sleep around, no questions asked, but if a woman makes nineteen or twenty mistakes she's a tramp.

—*Joan Rivers*

How do some men define Roe vs Wade? Two ways to cross a river.

—*Anonymous*

~

Don't kid yourself: telling a woman that you stopped by the local pub on your way home, but neglecting to mention that you spent the entire time with a teen model named Daphne in the back of her Jeep Cherokee is the same as telling a lie.

—*Barbara Graham,*
Women Who Run With the Poodles

This book is dedicated to Queen Isabella of Spain. Without her, the New World, and hence the Pittsburgh Steelers, the Hoover Dam and Ernest Hemingway, would not have been possible – and Christopher Columbus would have ended up sipping sangria and eating quiche in Lisbon. Naturally, he took all the credit.

—Joyce Jillson,
Real Women Don't Pump Gas

LOWLIFES

Eighty per cent of married men cheat in America. The rest cheat in Europe.

—*Jackie Mason*

~

Paula Jones is suing President Clinton for $700,000 for allegedly proposing she perform a sex act on him. In that case, every woman in America is owed millions by construction workers.

—*Elayne Boosler*

He was the most self-involved guy I ever met in my life. He had a coffee mug on his table that said, 'I'm the greatest'. He had a plaque on the wall that said, 'I'm number one'. And on his bedspread it said, 'The Best'. In the middle of making love he said, 'Move over – you're getting in my way'.

—*Karen Haber*

'I am not just another notch on your belt?' she asked him. 'Of course not,' he said as he put a mark on the chalkboard.

—Jay Leno

~

Outside every thin woman is a fat man trying to get in.

—Katherine Whitehorn

Whenever you want to marry someone, go have lunch with his ex-wife.

—*Shelley Winters*

~

A bachelor is a guy who leans toward women, but not far enough to lose his balance.

—*Anonymous*

Classic male excuse hall of fame: 'Don't take it personally.' 'I do love you as a friend.' 'But you never asked me if I was married with kids!' 'Our break-up has nothing to do with ____. (Put her name here.)' 'I just need some space.' '(I lied because) I didn't want to hurt your feelings.' 'It's not what you think . . .' 'I thought *you* were using birth control.'

—*Anonymous*

When this judge let a rapist go because the woman had been wearing a miniskirt and so was 'asking for it' I thought, 'Ladies, what we all should do is this: next time we see an ugly guy on the street, shoot him. After all, he knew he was ugly when he left the house. He was asking for it.'

—*Ellen Cleghorn*

~

We had a lot in common; I loved him and he loved him.

—*Shelley Winters*

In passing, also, I would like to say that the first time Adam had a chance he laid the blame on woman . . .

—*Nancy Astor,*
My Two Countries

~

When a man tells me he's going to put all his cards on the table, I always look up his sleeve.

—*Leslie Hore-Belisha*

I wasn't kissing her. I was whispering in her mouth.

—Chico Marx, when his wife caught him kissing a chorus girl

~

Women dream of world peace, a safe environment and eliminating hunger. What do men dream of? Being stuck in an elevator with the Doublemint twins.

—Anonymous

I had to hold down three jobs to put him through school. Then when I turned twenty-six and thought I should go back to college, he divorced me. For a nineteen-year-old bimbette with straw for brains who walks seven feet behind him so that when he stops to read a road map she wipes his butt. But I'm not bitter.

—*Diane Ford*

He was like a cock who thought the sun had risen to hear him crow.

—*George Eliot*

~

I just want him to call so I can tell him I never want to see him again.

—*Bill Cosby*

~

Why dogs are better than men: dogs mean it when they kiss you.

—*Anonymous*

The next morning, Crash was gone. It's not like it was the first time I'd gone to bed with a man and woke up with a note.

—*Ron Shelton,* Bull Durham

~

When a man is wrapped up in himself, he makes a pretty small package.

—*Ruskin*

TOTAL
SLAMS

Q: What's the difference between men and pigs?
A: Pigs don't get drunk and act like men.

—*Anonymous*

~

There are no great men, buster.
There are only men.

—*Charles Schnee,*
The Bad and The Beautiful

Ninety-nine per cent of men give the other 1 per cent a bad name.

—*Anonymous*

~

If they can put one man on the moon why can't they put them all there?

—*Chocolate Waters*

Have you ever wondered why men who haven't had a date in six months know what women really want?

—*Anonymous*

~

A man's home may seem to be his castle on the outside; inside it is more often his nursery.

—*Clare Boothe Luce*

You never see a man walking down
the street with a woman who has a
pot belly and a bald spot.

—*Elayne Boosler*

~

Can you imagine a world without
men? No crime and lots of happy
fat women.

—*Nicole Hollander*

If a man watches three football games in a row, he should be declared legally dead.

—*Erma Bombeck*

~

Announcing:
SEMINARS FOR MEN
COURSE 020:
You Too Can Be A Designated Driver

—*Anonymous*

Men! The only animal in the world to fear!

—*D.H. Lawrence*

~

Statistics show there are three ages when men misbehave: young, old and middle.

—*Anonymous*

History records only one
indispensable man: Adam.

—Anonymous

~

Why dogs are better than men: You
can train a dog.

—Anonymous

~

Some men grow; others just swell.

—Anonymous

When a male heckler called out, 'Are you a lesbian?' she immediately replied, 'Are you my alternative?'

—*Florynce Kennedy*

~

Not all guys are icky . . . I mean, look at Tom Cruise . . . but most of them are disgusting.

—*Anonymous*

What are two reasons why men don't mind their own business? No mind, no business.

—*Anonymous*

~

Have you ever wondered why men who aren't on speaking terms with their families know how to achieve peace in the Middle East?

—*Anonymous*

There are many words you could use to describe men today. You could say they are charming, strong, caring. . . . You would be wrong, but you could say them.

—*Anonymous*

~

Conceit is God's gift to little men.

—*Bruce Barton*

Talk to a man about himself and he will listen for hours.

—*Benjamin Disraeli*

~

I want a perfume that says to a man, 'Go to Hell!'

—*C. Sele, cartoon*

~

The only problem with women is men.

—*Kathie Sarachild*

GUYS ON GUYS

To get a man's attention, just stand in front of the TV and don't move. He'll talk to you. I promise.

—*Tim Allen*

~

The most difficult secret for a man to keep is his own opinion of himself.

—*Marcel Pagnol*

Shame is the feeling you have
when you agree with the woman
who loves you that you are the
man she thinks you are.

—*Carl Sandburg*

~

In love, women are professionals,
men are amateurs.

—*Francois Truffaut*

Men, in general, are but great children.

—*Napoleon*

~

I think it can be stated without denial that no man ever saw a man he would be willing to marry if he were a woman.

—*George Gibbs,*
How To Stay Married

The wedding is a beautiful thing. I
think the idea behind the tuxedo is
the woman's point of view that
'Men are all the same, we might as
well dress them that way'.

—*Jerry Seinfeld*

~

The same time that women came
up with PMS, men came up with
ESPN.

—*Blake Clark*

Sigmund Freud once said, 'What do women want?' The only thing I have learned in fifty-two years is that women want men to stop asking dumb questions like that.

—*Bill Cosby*

~

Being a woman is a terribly difficult task since it consists principally in dealing with men.

—*Joseph Conrad*

An American Monkey after getting
drunk on Brandy would never
touch it again, and thus is much
wiser than most men.

—*Charles Darwin*

~

There are two things no man will
admit he cannot do well: drive and
make love.

—*Stirling Moss*

When a young man complains that a young lady has no heart, it is a pretty certain sign that she has his.

—*George D. Prentice*

~

Any man who says he doesn't desire to have sex with a woman he thinks is attractive is lying.

—*Corbin Bernsen*

Men build bridges and throw railroads across deserts, and yet they contend successfully that the job of sewing on a button is beyond them. Accordingly, they don't have to sew buttons.

—*Heywood Broun*

~

Men get to be a mixture of the charming mannerisms of the women they have known.

—*F. Scott Fitzgerald,*
The Crack-Up

Most men do not mature, they simply grow taller.

—*Leo Rosten*

~

No man ever told a woman she talked too much when she was telling him how wonderful he is.

—*Earl Wilson*

Some women . . . enjoy tremendously being told they look a mess – and they actually thrill to the threat of physical violence. I've never met one that does, mind you, but they probably do exist. In books. By men.

—*Alan Ayckbourn,* Round and Round the Garden

Men never learn anything about women, but they have a lot of fun trying.

—Olin Miller

~

A man may be so totally lost to hope that he will refuse to believe he can ever do or be anything, but few ever get so far down that they can't imagine a woman might be in love with them.

—H.L. Davis

Guys start acting macho at an early age. Any parent will tell you that girl babies will generally display a wide-eyed curiosity about the world, whereas boy babies will generally try to destroy it.

—*Dave Barry*

Man today obviously needs work. Some need a kinder, more caring outlook. Some need a heightened appreciation of woman, his fellow creature on the planet whom he has been neglecting lately. Some men you just want to run up to and slap. Others have bad posture and poor eating habits. Man needs major work and I'm afraid it's going to be expensive.

—*Frank Gannon,*
All About Man

The rooster makes more racket
than the hen that lays the egg.

—*Joel Chandler Harris*

~

Whenever you see a man with
handkerchief, socks and tie to
match, you may be sure he is
wearing a present.

—*Frank Case*

The majority of husbands remind me of an orangutan trying to play the violin.

—*Balzac*

~

You know why men lie to women so much? Because women don't believe them anyway!

—*Roy Blount, Jr*

Men just don't say anything meaningful to each other unless they're really drunk. Sometimes while jogging together. It's tradition.

— *Peter Nelson*

~

There's only three types of men in the world: the loving, the faithful and the majority.

— *Richard Jeni*

Most men act so tough and strong
on the outside because on the
inside, we are scared, weak and
fragile. Men, not women, are the
weaker sex.

—*Jerry Rubin*, Chicago Tribune

THE
SECRET LIVES
OF MEN

What men really mean: 'It's a guy thing.' Really means . . . 'There is no rational thought pattern connected with it and you have no chance at all of making it logical.'

—*Anonymous*

~

Every man has a secret ambition to outsmart horses, fish and women.

—*Anonymous*

Women have one great advantage over men. It is commonly thought that if they marry they have done enough and need career no further. If a man marries, on the other hand, public opinion is all against him if he takes this view.

—*Rose Macaulay,*
A Casual Commentary

Remember when I told you that I didn't love you no more? Well I lied.

—*Robert Cray, 'Well I Lied'*

~

How many roads must a man travel down before he admits he's lost?

—*Anonymous*

Men can read maps better than women. 'Cause only the male mind could conceive of one inch equalling a hundred miles.

—*Roseanne*

~

I sleep with my teddy bear because I know where he's been.

—*Anonymous*

The man who has no secrets from his wife either has no secrets or no wife.

—*Anonymous*

~

The trouble with marriage is that, while every woman is at heart a mother, every man is at heart a bachelor.

—*E.V. Lucas*

Boys will be boys, and so will a lot of middle-aged men.

—*Kin Hubbard*

~

Men invented language to satisfy their deep need to complain.

—*Lily Tomlin*

Men thirty to thirty-nine years old think about sex every fifteen minutes. After forty, the frequency drops to once every half hour.

—Men's Health Magazine

~

Most accidents occur in the home. Many men use this as an excuse to stay out late.

—Anonymous

Few women admit their age. Few men act theirs.

—*Anonymous*

~

Why dogs are better than men: gorgeous dogs don't know they're gorgeous.

—*Anonymous*

Teenage boys who whistle at girls
are just going through a stage
which will probably last fifty years.

—*Anonymous*

~

Chivalry is a man's inclination to
defend a woman against every
man but himself.

—*Anonymous*

I've been asked when lying to a woman is okay. All the time would be just fine. As long as you don't get caught. Just don't get caught.

—*Tim Allen*

~

The intimate revelations of young men, or at least the terms in which they express them, are usually plagiaristic and marred by obvious suppressions.

—*F. Scott Fitzgerald,*
The Great Gatsby

The tragedy of machismo is that a man is never quite man enough.

—*Germaine Greer, 'My Mailer Problem'*, Esquire

~

A romantic man often feels more uplifted with two women than with one: his love seems to hit the ideal mark somewhere between two different faces.

—*Elizabeth Bowen,*
The Death of the Heart

Upscale young men seem to go for the kind of woman who plays with a full deck of credit cards, who won't cry when she's knocked to the ground while trying to board the six o'clock train and whose schedule doesn't allow for a sexual encounter lasting more than twelve minutes.

—*Barbara Ehrenreich,*
'The Cult of Busyness',
New York Times

Beware of men who cry. It's true that men who cry are sensitive to and in touch with their feelings, but the only feelings they tend to be sensitive to and in touch with are their own.

—*Nora Ephron,* Heartburn

~

When a man brings his wife flowers for no reason – there's a reason.

—*Molly McGee*

Never worry for fear you have broken a man's heart: at the worst it is only sprained and a week's rest will put it in perfect working order again.

—*Helen Rowland,*
Reflections of a Bachelor Girl

~

If there is anything disagreeable going on, men are always sure to get out of it. . . .

—*Jane Austen,*
Northanger Abbey

If a woman wears gay colours, rouge and a startling hat, a man hesitates to take her out. If she wears a little turban and a tailored suit, he takes her out and stares all evening at a woman in gay colours, rouge and a startling hat.

—Baltimore Beacon

~

Men are always ready to respect anything that bores them.

—*Marilyn Monroe*

What men really mean: 'Good idea.' Really means . . . 'It'll never work. And I'll spend the rest of the day gloating.'

—*Anonymous*

~

You men are unaccountable things; mad till you have your mistresses, and then stark mad till you are rid of 'em again.

—*John Vanbrugh*,
The Provoked Wife

There is nothing about which men lie so much as about their sexual powers. In this at least every man is, what in his heart he would like to be, a Casanova.

—*W. Somerset Maugham,*
A Writer's Notebook

~

He who believes in nothing still needs a girl to believe in him.

—*Eugen Rosenstock-Huessy*

To men, porno movies are beautiful love stories with all the boring stuff taken out.

—*Richard Jeni*

~

'Young' is an adjective used by men to describe a woman who is under eighteen or a man who is under eighty.

—*Nancy Linn-Desmond*

What remains a mystery about men? Their reticence. I mean, fling the door open and live your freakin' life. Feel your feelings. Be a man.

—*Ashley Judd, GQ*

~

Man to woman: 'You think I don't have any feelings! Well, lust counts as a feeling . . . doesn't it?'

—*Stephanie Piro*

Of course the single life has problems – having two lovers is a scheduling problem, and three is a real test of a man's organizational ability, and yet those are the very problems a man hopes for, Figaro.

—*Garrison Keillor,*
The Book of Guys

~

Men like to barbecue. Men will cook if danger is involved.

—*Rita Rudner*

Wouldn't it be great if you could just be honest with a woman you find attractive and say, 'Hi. I'm Bob. You're very attractive. Want to go home and rut like weasels?'

—*Tim Allen*

~

Women love cats. Men say they love cats, but when women aren't looking, men kick cats.

—*Matt Groening*

A survey was taken on the nocturnal habits of men. The results showed that 5 per cent of the men get up to drink a glass of water, 10 per cent to go to the bathroom, and 85 per cent get up to go home.

—*Joe Uris,* Say It Again,
ed. Dorothy Uris

~

Men love to talk about politics, but they often forget to do political things such as voting.

—*Anonymous*

Men can't know what it's like to be pregnant, and women can't know what it's like to have an organ which is half voluntary, half involuntary. We're in a much better position to understand penises than you are, and we don't even know what's going on, sometimes.

—*Peter Nelson*

To a woman, having flowers sent to her is thoughtful. To a man, sending flowers is a way of being thoughtful without putting any thought into it. It's like foreign aid.

—*Roy Blount, Jr*

~

Interesting: a word a man uses to describe a woman who lets him do all the talking.

—*Anonymous*

Announcing:
SEMINARS FOR MEN
COURSE 021:
Honest – You Don't Look Like
Mel Gibson – Especially Naked

—*Anonymous*

~

Girls are always running through
my mind. They don't dare walk.

—*Andy Gibb*

THE
SEX PART

How can you tell if a man is sexually excited? He's breathing.

—*Anonymous*

~

Men are those creatures with two legs and eight hands.

—*Jayne Mansfield*

If men really knew how to do it,
they wouldn't have to pay for it.

—*Roseanne*

~

Dr Ruth says we women should
tell our lovers how to make love to
us. My boyfriend goes nuts if I tell
him how to drive!

—*Pam Stone*

The male attitude toward sex is like squirting jam into a doughnut.

—*Germaine Greer*

~

A lot of guys think the larger a woman's breasts are, the less intelligent she is. I don't think it works like that. I think it's the opposite. I think the larger a woman's breasts are, the less intelligent the men become.

—*Anita Wise*

An Irishman is the only man in the world who will step over the bodies of a dozen naked women to get to a bottle of stout.

—*Anonymous*

~

A man's sexuality goes through three stages: tri-weekly, try-weekly, and try-weakly.

—*Sydnie Meltzer Kleinhenz*

Snuggle: an act of warmth that
your husband will inevitably
interpret as foreplay.

—*Tom Carey*

~

Why dogs are better than men:
dogs understand what 'no' means.

—*Anonymous*

Condoms should be marketed in three sizes, jumbo, colossal and super colossal, so that men do not have to go in and ask for the small.

—*Barbara Seaman*

~

By keeping men off, you keep them on.

—*Gay*

He doesn't want to take a girl out and do things – he'd rather take her in and undo things.

—*Anonymous*

~

What men really mean: 'I was listening to you. It's just that I have things on my mind.' Really means . . . 'I was wondering if that red-head over there is wearing a bra.'

—*Anonymous*

Women complain about sex more than men. Their gripes fall into two major categories: (1) Not enough. (2) Too much.

—*Ann Landers*

~

Women prefer 30–40 minutes of foreplay. Men prefer 30–40 seconds of foreplay. Men consider driving back to her place as part of the foreplay.

—*Matt Groening*

If love is blind, why are so many men attracted to a beautiful woman?

—*Anonymous*

~

Most men have a way with women, but it's seldom their own.

—*Anonymous*

'Please, I'll only put it in for a minute.' She replies with, 'What does he think I am, a microwave?'

—*Beverly Mickins*

~

Give a man a free hand and he'll run it all over you.

—*Mae West*

The clothes that keep a man looking his best are worn by girls on beaches.

—Walter Woerner

~

If half the engineering effort and public interest that go into the research on the American bosom had gone into our guided-missile programme, we would now be running hot-dog stands on the moon.

—Al Capp

I've always resisted the notion that there is canine in every guy, and yet that sure would explain a few things, not the least of which is this oxymoron: Pamela Anderson, 'actress'.

—*Leonard Pitts, Jr*

~

What a man enjoys about a woman's clothes are his fantasies of how she would look without them.

—*Brendan Francisin,*
1,911 Best Things Anybody Ever Said

Why don't men often show their true feelings? Because they don't have any.

— *Anonymous*

~

Why do so many women fake orgasm? Because so many men fake foreplay.

— *Anonymous*

Fondle the woman in your life
once for every thousand times you
play with your private parts. That
should be just about right.

—*Barbara Graham*

~

Woman, observing that her mate
went out of his way to make
himself entertaining, rightly
surmised that sex had something to
do with it.

—*E.B. White,*
The Sexual Revolution

He gave her a look that you could have poured on a waffle.

—*Ring Lardner*

~

Men in lust aren't interested in quality.

—*Peter Nelson*

A woman isn't just a collection of buttons for a man to press, a collection of erotic knee jerks.

—*Camille Cosby*

~

We live in far too permissive a society. Never before has pornography been this rampant. And those films are lit so badly!

—*Woody Allen*

I'm in love . . . I mean, this guy is so sweet, he even kisses me before we do it.

—*Laura Kightlinger*

~

I suspect your version of romance is whatever'll separate me from my panties.

—*Laurian Leggett,*
  Doc Hollywood

Easy: a term used to describe a woman who has the sexual morals of a man.

—Anonymous

~

Announcing:
SEMINARS FOR MEN
COURSE 014:
How To Stay Awake After Sex

—Anonymous

What's a man's idea of foreplay? A half hour of begging.

—*Anonymous*

~

Men and women can never be friends because the sex part gets in the way.

—*Nora Ephron,*
When Harry Met Sally

FEAR
OF THE
'C' WORD

If you want to scare your boyfriend next Halloween, come dressed as what he fears most. Commitment.

—*Peter Nelson,*
Real Man Tells All

~

A woman feels a man's love should be like a toothbrush. It shouldn't be shared.

—*Anonymous*

A man's heart is like a sponge –
soaked with emotion and
sentiment. He can squeeze out a
little bit for every pretty woman he
meets.

—*Anonymous*

~

Apparently men rarely dream
about getting married. Well, that
figures. Women have a magazine
called *Bride*, but there's no
magazine for men called *Groom*.

—*Mary Reinholz*

A girl's hardest task is to prove to a man that his intentions are serious.

—*Helen Rowland*

~

Men do not settle down. Men surrender.

—*Chris Rock*

Guys are born with a fundamental, genetically transmitted mental condition known to psychologists as: The Fear That If You Get Attached to a Woman, Some Unattached Guy, Somewhere, Will Be Having More Fun Than You.

—*Dave Barry*

~

They call him the 'Dry Cleaner' – he works fast and leaves no ring.

—*Anonymous*

'I can't tell you how much I love you', he said. 'Try,' she said. 'I'm very fond of you,' he said. 'Nice try,' she said.

—*Charles Schulz*

~

Some men think that being married to a woman means merely seeing her in the mornings instead of in the evenings.

—*Helen Rowland*

'Geographically undesirable' is a term used by a man to describe a woman who is not a good dating prospect because she is either more than a fifteen-minute drive away or else lives near enough to see what time he comes home and with whom.

—Nancy Linn-Desmond

To a woman the words 'I love you' represent a heartfelt expression of the intensely fond feelings you have for her. At least, this kind of thing will be what the woman has in mind when she utters the words, and so she will not be pleased if your response is 'thank you' or 'I know'.

—*Merrill Markoe*

A man does not call a relationship a relationship – he refers to it as 'that time when me and Suzie were bonking on a semi-regular basis'.

—*Matt Groening*

~

Announcing:
SEMINARS FOR MEN
COURSE 008:
Parenting – It Doesn't End With Conception

—*Anonymous*

'I'm sorry,' guys are always telling women, 'but I'm just not ready to make a commitment.' Guys are in a permanent state of nonreadiness. If guys were turkey breasts, you could put them in a 350-degree oven on July Fourth, and they still wouldn't be done in time for Thanksgiving.

—Dave Barry

CAN'T
LiVE WiTH
'EM . . .

Men are the enemy, but I still love the enemy.

—*Cameron Crowe,*
Jerry McGuire

~

There are men I could spend eternity with. But not this life.

—*Kathleen Norris,*
The Middle of the World

Q: When did God create men?
A: When she realized that vibrators couldn't dance or buy drinks.

—*Anonymous*

~

The male is a domestic animal which, if treated with firmness and kindness, can be trained to do most things.

—*Jilly Cooper*

If you haven't had at least a slight poetic crack in the heart, you have been cheated by nature. Because a broken heart is what makes life so wonderful five years later, when you see the guy in an elevator and he is fat and smoking a cigar and saying, 'Long time no see'.

—*Phyllis Batelle,*
New York Journal-American

Announcing:
SEMINARS FOR MEN
COURSE 022:
The Obtainable Goal – Omitting
"/@#* From Your Vocabulary

—*Anonymous*

~

For though I know he loves me
Tonight my heart is sad
His kiss was not so wonderful
As all the dreams I had.

—*Sara Teasdale*

When women go wrong, men go right after them.

—Mae West

~

Whenever I date a guy, I think, is this the man I want my children to spend their weekends with?

—Rita Rudner

Many men are slow but sure.
Others are just slow.

—*Anonymous*

~

If a man tells a woman she's
beautiful, she'll overlook most of
his other lies.

—*Anonymous*

Q: What do you do when your boyfriend walks out?
A: Shut the door.

—*Angela Martin*

~

My mother's two categories: nice men did things for you, bad men did things to you.

—*Margaret Atwood,* Lady Oracle

Sure I want a man in my life, but not in my house. I want him to hook up the VCR and leave. Why should I want him in the house?

—*Joy Behar*

~

You have to kiss an awful lot of frogs before you get a prince.

—*Graffito*

They say that men suffer
As badly, as long
I worry, I worry
In case they are wrong.

—Wendy Cope, 'I Worry'

~

Men: can't live without 'em, can't
leave 'em by the side of the road.

—Anonymous

I like the concept of 'men' . . . It's
the reality I have problems with!

—*Stephanie Piro,* Fair Game

~

Bumper sticker: life's too short to
dance with ugly men.

—*Anonymous*

Good dates don't necessarily make good mates.

—*Barnett Brickner,*
A Treasury of the Art of Living

~

Though love can make the world go round, it often makes the world go flat.

—*Margaret Fishback,*
'I Stand Corrected'

You're not one of those women who tries to fix men, are you? Because men cannot be fixed.

—*Ron Shelton,* Tin Cup

~

It's always boys . . . that's all you want in high school. I don't care how old you get, it's still boys.

—*Sandra Bullock*

Reasons we like men just the way they are: they're enthusiastic about our bodies, even when we're not.

They're at peace with their bodies, except for maybe some minor anxiety over height, baldness, and/or penis size.

Their unapologetic lust for a nice hunk of beef or chocolate cake.

Their genuine ardour for tinkering with toilets, changing oil and assembling gas grills – jobs any intelligent woman can do but would be nuts to volunteer for.

How awestruck they are in the face of a Wonderbra or a homemade cookie.

—*Anonymous*

To all my boyfriends – past, present, and future: I love you. I hate you. I miss you. I want my money back. Choose the one that applies to you.

—*Kim Coles*

~

'I hate men!' she says as she goes back for more.

—*Katie Shulte*

POCKET
BOOKS

THE LITTLE BOOK OF
COMPLETE BOLLOCKS

Alistair Beaton

The only book in the entire universe that
can solve every single problem in your
life – for only £2.99. Alistair Beaton takes
on the therapy culture and invites you
to make friends with your anxiety and
give your anger a hug.

PRICE £2.99

ISBN 0 671 03767 6

POCKET
BOOKS

THE LITTLE BOOK OF MANAGEMENT BOLLOCKS

Alistair Beaton

Read this book and Alistair Beaton will
transform you overnight into a
successful modern manager, capable of
talking authentic management bollocks
on any given occasion, because, let's
face it, talking bollocks is what modern
management is all about.

PRICE £2.99
ISBN 0 7434 0413 0

**POCKET
BOOKS**

THE LITTLE BOOK OF
NEW LABOUR
BOLLOCKS

Alistair Beaton

Learn to survive in Blair's Britain with
this witty onslaught on the culture of
spin. Alistair Beaton takes on the might
of Millbank and reveals the bollocks
behind the soundbites.

PRICE £2.99

ISBN 0 7434 0412 2

**POCKET
BOOKS**

THE LITTLE BOOK OF
PSEUD FOOD

Sue Chef

Tossing the exotic fruit coulis and beds
of highly-bred lettuce aside, Sue Chef
presents us with some hilarious and
piognant truths about our love of all
things edible.

PRICE £2.99

ISBN 0 7434 3012 3